G000271424

There Will Be No More Nonsense

LORRAINE MARINER was born in 1974 and lives in London, where she works at the Poetry Library at the Southbank Centre. *Furniture* was shortlisted for the Forward Prize for Best First Collection and the Seamus Heaney Centre Poetry Prize.

Lorraine Mariner

There Will Be
No More Nonsense

PICADOR

First published 2014 by Picador
an imprint of Pan Macmillan, a division of Macmillan Publishers Limited
Pan Macmillan, 20 New Wharf Road, London N1 9RR
Basingstoke and Oxford
Associated companies throughout the world
www.panmacmillan.com

ISBN 978-1-4472-5394-5

9 8 7 6 5 4 3 2 1

A CIP catalogue record for this book is available from the British Library.

Printed and bound by CPI Group (UK) Ltd, Croydon, CR0 4YY

Visit **www.picador.com** to read more about all our books
and to buy them. You will also find features, author interviews and
news of any author events, and you can sign up for e-newsletters
so that you're always first to hear about our new releases.

For my mother

Acknowledgements

Acknowledgements are due to the editors of the following publications in which some of these poems have appeared: *Alaska Quarterly Review*, *Best American Poetry Blog*, *The Best British Poetry 2011*, *Domestic Cherry*, *Forest Poets Four*, *Granta (Online)*, *Live Canon Anthology 2012*, *The Missing Slate*, *The Moth*, *Neon Highway*, *New Welsh Review*, *Poetry Review*, *Rain of Poems London 2012*, *The Rialto*, *Where Rockets Burn Through: Contemporary Science Fiction Poems*.

Thank you to Annie Freud and the Whitechapel Gallery, who commissioned the poems 'Meeting the psychiatrist's wife' and 'Strangers' for the event *Paint into Words: Everybody Wants Everything*, held at the Whitechapel in response to the Alice Neel exhibition *Painted Truths*.

'The Grand Orrery' was written after eighteenth-century Grand Orreries in the Whipple Museum, Cambridge and the Royal Observatory Greenwich, and 'Memento mori' was written after an eighteenth-century mori pendant in the Wellcome Collection, London. Both poems were published in the anthology *Pocket Horizon* (Valley Press, 2013). Thank you to Kelley Swain, who commissioned these poems, and to everyone involved in the project.

I would like to acknowledge Nektarios Oraiopoulos, John Thalassinos and previous translators of Cavafy for help in translating 'As much as you can' and 'When they come alive'.

'Conversation at midnight' includes text from Edna St. Vincent Millay's introduction to *Conversation at Midnight* (New York: Harper & Brothers Publishers, 1937).

'God's Own Junkyard' was inspired by a video interview by Neil Meads with Neon Artist Chris Bracey on the BBC News website.

With very special thanks for friendship and inspiration to my first readers the Nevada Street Poets: Mick Delap, Malene Engelund, Dominic McLoughlin, David Nash, Kelley Swain and Sarah Westcott; to my colleagues at the Poetry Library, especially Pascal O'Loughlin, and to my editor Don Paterson, who gets the final word.

Contents

And then there will be no more nonsense

And then there will be no more nonsense
and you will tell her about that evening

when you stopped in the dusk at the edge
of the grass you had cut that afternoon

and looked back to where you had just sat
on the patio eating the meal she had cooked

and saw how blessed it all appeared if someone
had watched from where you stood.

Meeting the psychiatrist's wife

After Alice Neel's painting
'Psychiatrist's Wife (Elsie Rubin)', 1957

The psychiatrist's wife
has a dress the colour
of that bottle of claret
you shouldn't have drunk
last night. Has gold,
a pearl, a ruby ring
that resembles a sweet
that seems to be suggesting
you take, eat, but her hair
swept up in a directional
peak, is that telling you
to get lost? You would
swear her right hand
is carefully considering
what you have to say
but her left hand hidden
beneath the snow white
circular table, why –
that could be up to
all manner of things.

The Deadly Sins and the Holy Virtues – No. 1 Chastity

The highlight of the morning I'd spent playing at Jenny's had been a perfume she'd recently been given in a bottle shaped like a mermaid. I'd been bowled over by this moulded glass beauty; her lush contoured hair, her nippleless breasts.

I'd gone home to find my mother had been shopping and bought me a notebook. Though it was lined there was nothing I wanted to write down. Instead, I drew a naked woman – with nipples – in profile (a little bit Picasso, though I was still to meet Picasso in *The Great Artists* weekly partwork my parents would collect in the future).

When I showed my nude to my mother she was taken by surprise, unaware that earlier in the day I'd been marvelling at a topless mermaid. My bohemianism was quickly curtailed. By teatime my drawing had clothes.

Fortune

I told my mother
about the fortune cookie
I'd had with a take-away
the night before, how it said
You will be very happy tomorrow
and she laughed, really laughed,
in a way she doesn't normally
and it made me very happy.

The Grand Orrery

My master's study holds the Universe
and when he has business in town
Mrs Johnson, the housekeeper, has the key

and she lets me in to wax the leather
on his desk, and dust the books that fill
the shelves, and finally I polish the planets.

There is a bronze sphere in the centre,
that's the Sun, a green and blue bauble
which is the Earth, where we live,

and next to it a pearl on a stick that looks
like a lady's hatpin – why, that's the Moon.
And there are more hatpins and more baubles

for ours is not the only Moon and not the only
World that goes around the Sun. Mr Johnson
taught me all this. He has served drinks

to the master and his friends and seen
the Orrery wound up and set in motion.
The master put a lamp in the place of the Sun

and the planets turned in their circles.
I would give my eye teeth to see such a thing.
I told Mr Johnson I wished I was him

and Mrs Johnson said I was too much like
my star sign, the Lion, painted on the side
of that infernal contraption and she made me

stand out in the cold on the kitchen step,
which I had scrubbed that very morning,
to take a good long look at the real Moon.

February

What does that bird
have to sing about
at 3.30 in the morning?

It is pitch dark
and minus one degree.
Is he remembering green?

Is his tiny mind
telling him that soon
this tree will once again

be green? *Oh green!*
Green, green, green.
Recollect with me.

The Deadly Sins and the Holy Virtues – No. 2 Gluttony

Origin: Latin "gluttire", meaning to gulp down or swallow

We didn't stand a chance, my siblings and I, when it came to loving tea. Here's our mum giving us a milky weak version in a tippy cup while we sit in a high chair. Now we're old enough to sleep in a bed and here's our dad with a mug of tea come to wake us up.

But how did we get from a morning ritual and a cup sometimes of an evening (and always on a Sunday after lunch) to this; some tea bell which cannot be ignored ringing in our taste buds at two-hourly intervals?

It was a revelation when I got to university to discover that some people could leave for lectures in the morning without a drop having passed their lips. And those nights when their heart had just got broken in five places but no, no thank you, they wouldn't like a cup of tea.

Tell me
Everything
Amber

Waterloo East

On one of those mornings
when I felt like resigning
from my life, I could see

the appeal of dressing
like the woman walking ahead
of me along the platform

who had two sequined cats
wearing heart-shaped lockets
appliquéd on the back

of her jacket, or like the woman
coming towards me in peach
leggings and a cardigan

that resembled candyfloss;
of dressing like you might not
be able to tie the ribbons

that were your shoelaces,
of looking like you might just
eat yourself for brunch.

O$_2$, North Greenwich

There is much to be thankful for
in this part of town, not least
those times at North Greenwich station

when you might be going down
and they are coming up the escalators
in their hundreds, to a concert,

some looking fabulous, some
in identifying t-shirts, and you can
almost touch the expectation

and good feeling: for how could they not
be happy surrounded by those
who love what they love?

Ie ie ie yadi yader

Not streetlight or carlight
but moonlight woke me
the night before I saw
Lene Lovich in concert
in her sixty-fifth year.

I woke with my head
in a pool of full moon
and I was very afraid
for my brain was filled
with Lene from YouTube

(*Top of the Pops*
nineteen-seventy-nine,
in a kaftan, a headdress,
with fairytale braids, making
otherworldly vocals,

making big staring eyes)
and her theory of lyrics
that I'd read on a fansite,
if you can't find the words
then just make a noise.

If I went back to sleep
would I wake in the morning
with a new lucky number,
with plaits to my waist,
would I

                    uh
        Uh   oh!
            oh

Toll booth attendant

It might look
like the worst job
on earth
sitting in a booth
on a motorway
collecting money
so a car
can go over
a bridge

but the snatches
of music
you would hear
as the windows
roll down
and back up –

somebody's
favourite
driving song,
a sonata,
a hit played
on Radio 2
caught in
intermittent
blasts

or suddenly
something
you have never
heard before
so beautiful
that your soul
begins to lift

then it's gone
foot down
crossing the river

The Deadly Sins and the Holy Virtues – No. 3 Charity

For weeks at Brownies we'd been making peppermints and constructing woven paper baskets in which to present them to the residents of the Hall Lane Nursing Home. Brown Owl's mother, Tawny Owl, had also been teaching us music hall songs; *It's a Long Way to Tipperary*, *Who Were You With Last Night*, *Where Did You Get That Hat*, *My Old Man Said Follow the Van*...

But not even the Brownie who'd been there previously and whispered about the smell of wee, visiting a lady she wouldn't admit to being her grandma, had prepared us for our reception. We were used to grandparents, who when they couldn't come to our dance school shows, insisted we perform them (with costume changes) in their living rooms; who listened to us playing our recorders down the telephone. I thought the old people here, who dropped our sweets and didn't applaud, hated us. And while we sang those songs I was as lost as they were, wearing a brown bobble hat no one could ever envy, not yet understanding about infidelity or what it was to live in a home you could no longer afford.

Credit

There is a beautiful symmetry in the fact
that my friend who rents a Peabody flat
just behind Oxford Street has a pet guinea pig

who pisses on the shredded-up bank statements
and till receipts donated by her work colleagues.
And sometimes I gather my own shredding

and go and visit them, hold Milo in my hands
until his tiny legs start windmilling,
desperate to get back to the bottom of his cage.

Austerity measures

We tightened our belts
but still our trousers
dragged on the pavement
tripping us up.

Monkey

You came back to me today
after 30 years when from
his swivel chair my colleague
offered peanuts still in their shells
to me in my swivel chair.

Suddenly I was back
with my top school infant class
standing in front of your cage
to watch you squatting
on your branch, chewing your food,
which you then decided to spit at us.

You hit our teacher
who found you hilarious.
You also hit me and that evening
my mother spent what seemed
like an hour combing
congealed nut out of my hair.

Belligerent monkey,
my colleague has got peanut husks
all over the carpet around his desk
and tomorrow morning
before we arrive, somebody
from another country
will hoover them up.

Love in a time of economic uncertainty

Friday
Standing in a bar after work,
her second glass of pinot grigio.
Overwhelming urge to stroke
team leader's cheek.

Monday
Enquires after team leader's weekend.
Reply involves tightness
of quad muscles following long distance
road race. Overwhelming need
to cook team leader a Full English Breakfast
before driving him to next running meet.

Tuesday
Becomes convinced team leader
deliberately touched her fingers
whilst returning a spreadsheet
that isn't adding up.

Wednesday
Becomes convinced team leader
is scanning her face for the answer
to some fundamental question
while asking if she'd like a cup of tea.

Thursday
Watches as co-worker talks to team leader
and team leader's attention is drawn back
to computer screen indicating
that this discussion has now ended.
Makes herself imagine various permutations
of this in a domestic setting.

Friday
Decides to memorise the colour
of all of her work colleagues' eyes.

Factory

So I tried to shut
that factory down

laid off
all those operatives

who'd been working
in my head non-stop

constructing
your good name

explained that times
were hard

and my heart
was even harder.

Disassembly
wasn't as easy

as I'd imagined:
they formed a union

turned up as usual
the next day

said they'd accept
a three day week

half-pay
insisted this

was the best job
they'd ever had.

The Deadly Sins and the Holy Virtues – No. 4 Sloth

At fifteen my resourceful friend, who'd progressed from a paper round to working *in* the paper shop, diversified into waitressing across the high street at Lyn's Pantry, but deciding it wasn't for her, put me forward for the job. When I got it I was ecstatic. This was the big time; £12 a Saturday and whatever I wanted to eat for lunch. I soon discovered I hated waitressing as much as my friend did – froze with teenage embarrassment as I took the orders, flustered over making the drinks and snacks. So I let the other girls waitress and opted to stay in the kitchen, washing-up.

When my mother and sister came to visit, Lyn persuaded me to go out front and serve them. I decided they could do without the frivolity of cress and took them their order of prawn sandwiches without it. I didn't think they'd notice but I must have once described to them the process of making sandwiches at Lyn's Pantry; how we cut them into four triangles, then placed two pointing upwards, two pointing outwards on a napkin on the plate, the final touch a sprinkling of cress across the top. I can still see the disappointment on their faces, the nakedness suddenly of the bread. If my mother left me a tip I've no recollection.

An apple for Bathsheba

I remember when I first realised
I was beautiful. The grocer
handing change to my mother

stared at my mouth as I bit
the apple and my mother slapped
my hand so the apple fell into

the dirt; grabbed my arm
when I bent to pick it up,
pulled me towards home.

A monolith for Lot's Wife

Though it was
an angel
that took her
by the hand
and led her
from her house
still she had
to look back
to where its
columns burned
so she was turned
into a pillar
herself
monumental
until the day
the rains came
nostalgia
seasoning
the soil

Monochrome

Did I never wonder why adults hadn't told me
where they were the day everything went colour?
Perhaps I took my answer from the fact
that in the seventies there were an awful lot
of avocado bathroom suites.

But to have such faith in old films and photographs
and believe the world had only recently developed!
Teenagers sending messages from their smartphones
must think that in the dark days of landlines
we had nothing to say.

We two against the world

For Nicky

We two against the world
with your camera.
No need for a passerby
when you've got Self Time
and a bench or a stile
to prop it on and a taste
for the will-you-won't-you
make it to my side
before the shutter goes.

140 characters

Your brain may dribble out of your ears and this town is full of tightly dressed women with Twitter accounts so do not get drunk without me.

As much as you can

After Cavafy

And if you cannot live the life you want,
try this one at least
as much as you can: do not embarrass it
in all the conglomeration of the world,
in all the rushing and the patter.

Do not embarrass it by dragging it
around and exposing it,
in the daily madness
of meetings and networking,
until its strangeness weighs you down.

What else to do

In reply

And I could not live the life I wanted
but I did not know
what else to do: so I posted
the best bits on the World Wide Web
for everyone to see.

And they liked it;
so then I tweeted every thought
that came into my head,
and my life became a strutting peacock
pecking at my heels.

Strangers

Those people who talk
to strangers
who make eye contact
with absolutely anyone –

their souls have a lid
perhaps or lashes
some form of protection
because most people

are not to be trusted
and how do they cope
with the brightness
when they are?

Domestic interior

WORRY

It is white.
It vibrates
at intervals.
It has two doors.
Behind the smaller door

there is ice.
Sometimes I cannot close
the smaller door
and have to eat
what's in there.

GRIEF

It can be lifted
with one hand.
It has three different
heat settings
represented
by one, two, or three
black dots.
It has a button
which you press
to squirt water
on to deep creases.

I use mine every week
but I know people
who only use theirs
on formal occasions.

LOVE

It is a plastic coated steel frame
consisting of very thin poles.
If it was only steel
it would rust on your clothes.

Depending on its size
it has the capacity
to hold one or two loads
but it is embarrassing,
if you live in one room
as I do, to have this on display
when visitors come.

If visitors do come
it can be folded flat
and put out of sight.

The Deadly Sins and the Holy Virtues – No. 5 Patience

Our mother had too much faith in us that December, thought my brother and I could share the Father Christmas advent calendar with plastic figures waiting behind the doors on his stomach, with his legs that leapt for joy when we pulled a string. We'd longed for him – state of the art, owned last year by the coolest kids – bought to appease us for the birth of our sister.

Two weeks in and we couldn't remember whose turn it was to open today's door, started bickering. Our sleep deprived mother went ballistic; tore Santa in two so we could have half each, miniature pixies scattering across the kitchen. I was still sobbing when our lift to school knocked at the door.

Coming home that afternoon I'd forgotten the events of the morning until I encountered Santa in his place on the fridge, Scotch Tape around his belly, keepsakes back behind the bent doors, my sister asleep in the warmth of our mother's cooking. So we started over, with our reassembled, paralysed Santa, counting the days until Christmas.

Appliances

I always seem to have had a surfeit of moisture,
anxious palms, eyes on the brink, but in this studio flat
I live too closely to my household appliances –
sleep to the hum of a fridge – for the electricity
you have been generating which cannot be plugged in.
A fuse blew when I ironed, the microwave declines
to rotate, then my last-legged washing machine spun
so hard on its final round I thought it was going to bore
down through the wood-effect linoleum. At night
I release my mattress from the wall and listen
to the calls of the brittle-boned oppidan foxes,
those scraggy embers who know how to demand
what must be supplied. I switch off the bathroom light
and the extractor fan begins to whine. If I could just be
closed into this folding bed, left until I'm dry.

And if we cried

at least our tears
were warm.

Desire

Here I go again
barking up
the wrong tree.

May these apples
fall on my head
and knock some
sense into me.

Dinner party acceptance

So I prayed that I would hit it off
with your girlfriend. That over the course
of an evening I would grow to like her more
than I liked you. That it would be hilarious,
one of the best nights of her life
thanks to me. That I could be cured.

Putting things into perspective at Gleirscher Alm

In Innsbruck I stood on a mountain
wearing borrowed ski pants
then sat on a one-person sled

raced to the bottom,
did it again,
and said to myself

'The one I love that
I should not love is not
a mountain, *this* is a mountain'

but back home in my flat grey city
my love was still blue blue skies
and endless white to me.

When they come alive

After Cavafy

Try to safeguard them, poet,
even though only a few can be kept,
your visions of those you desire.
Put them, half-hidden, in your lines.
Try to preserve them, poet,
whenever they come back to life in your mind
at night or during the shine of the midday.

They never told me

In reply

I did hold on to them, poet,
my visions of those I desired
and some were stronger than the others.
I put them, half-hidden, in my poems
just like you said. But I longed for my loves
to read my lines and recognise themselves.
If they did they never told me.

A bed of paper

On reflection

In the dead of night
in the heat of midday
a bed of paper
is no place to sleep.

Memento mori

Not for these times
a tiny skeleton rising
from his golden coffin,
hung around your neck,
to remind you that this life
is only temporary.

Instead, from the rolling
stacks of the library
I am sending you a photocopy
of my wrist on every page
of the yellowing article
you requested, which references
this mori pendant.

I imagine you at your desk
in another city, your dark head
bending to read and there
is my flesh, a spectre haunting
the bottom of the paper.

See how fragile my wrist,
with its branching veins
and looping creases,
appears alongside
the hard lines of the journal,
whose volumes stretch back
over a hundred years.

I held the book on the glass,
pressed 'Copy', and the words
of the dead scholar
and the blood in my ulnar artery
flooded momentarily
with artificial light.

When I folded these sheets
into their envelope
they were still warm.

The Deadly Sins and the Holy Virtues –
No. 6 Envy

The week the Children's Christian Crusade came to our church, I already had the love of Jesus, but what I really needed was a pop-a-point pencil embossed with the fact in gold letters and a sheet of bible verse stickers. My sister, Gemma, had won these items at Tuesday's meeting in the daily Under-Sevens Colouring Competition. Now, all I had to do was beat two hundred other children in the Seven to Eleven category.

Thursday, after school, sensing that time was against me, I had a flash of inspiration. Behind the steam train and words *Jesus Christ has paid the price for your ticket to heaven, all aboard!* I drew wavy lines in rainbow formation. Adding my picture to the pile that evening I was feeling confident but queasy, unable to join in the song *God's Not Dead* with my usual conviction; I had caught a bug from among the multitude and spent Friday home from school throwing up. Too ill to attend the final meeting, when I won, Gemma got to go up on stage for a second time to collect my prize.

But I still had my moment of glory. I got my mother to repeat several times the way the leader of the CCC called out my name. And before that there had been my sister, running to my sickbed, bringing me the good news.

When my brother broke

When my brother broke my Beverley doll –
who I loved more fiercely than I ever loved
my longed for "Pink and Pretty" Barbie, with a love
that only the second-rate can inspire – he hid it
behind his desk, terrified of how I'd react.
I'd left her on the settee when I went to bed
for my brother to absentmindedly maim,
fiddling with her leg, whilst watching
a TV series I was deemed too young for.
She was wedged there and looked for
for over a week, like the other woman
most homes will hide at some point. And while
I was not yet ready to put such childish things
away, did my brother suspect even then
I would never own such hair, such breasts,
that given half a chance I would take his desk?

Mermaid

Whip tail
hip jail
nowhere to go
but the sea.

These shells
on my breasts
are my breasts

oh sailor
the song
that I wail
is for me.

Millbank Penitentiary

It's my lunch hour so I head for the Tate
to look at that painting I like of Ophelia
drowning in the lake but I'm distracted
by the Damien Hirst spot boat docking
and cross the road to get a better look
narrowly avoiding a horse and cart.
I'm not wearing my good blue suit anymore
but what can only be described as coarse pyjamas
and my bare feet are not touching tarmac
but earth and I've just stepped in a puddle.
I'm also having trouble walking which might be
because my ankles are chained together
and I lift my hand up grasping the arm
of the man in front as I pitch forward
and realise my wrists are also chained.
The man behind says *Careful son!*
as we start walking on sloping wood.
If I look down I can see the river
between the planks and when I look up
I see a sail and think how I've never seen
a boat with a sail on the Thames before.
I look over my shoulder to find the Tate
obscured by a huge wall and the man
behind who seems to like me says
No good ever comes from looking back.
Get ready to meet the new world my friend
and I'm trying to fit my feet on wooden steps
as I descend into the ship's dark belly.

Day trip to Calais

For Mick Delap on his 70th Birthday

My maiden voyage
when I was seven
was a major disappointment.

Why had we crossed
the ocean to a place
resembling Romford?

Conversation at midnight

after Edna St. Vincent Millay

Before coming north after winter in Florida
I had decided to visit the islands of Sanibel
and Captiva, to look for seashells, of which
there are some very fine examples to be found
on those beaches. Have I never told you
about my passion for seashells? Some artists
I have known use mussel shells instead of a palette
to hold their paints, and in Greenwich Village
I was acquainted with a Surrealist who mixed
her pigments in the shell of an oyster. I arrived
at the Palm Hotel an hour or so before sunset,
engaged a room, and had my luggage sent up.
I did not go up to the room, not even to change
out of my travelling suit. I went out at once
upon the beach to gather shells. Looking back
a few moments later, holding in my hand
three rather charming seashells, I saw the hotel
in flames. There was nothing for it but to stand
beside a kitchen porter, our backs to the setting sun,
and watch as the Palm Hotel burned down,
destroying the manuscript of my recently completed
verse drama *Conversation at Midnight*.

At this hour

For Mia and Kristen

The way we play a game of Scrabble
is like that theory about how an animal
grows to fit its cage. First we played
one evening, then we started in the afternoon,
now we give over entire days
and I am ruined for all other opponents
who look at their watches, who at this hour
would put the word 'Home' down anywhere.

The Deadly Sins and the Holy Virtues – No. 7 Humility

It had been a fraught shopping trip, looking for a new swimming costume with my mother. After going into every possible shop in Romford we found ourselves at the Market where she lost her temper and no longer crying, I settled on a burnished gold fake Speedo.

Modelling the costume at home for my sister, she thought it was maybe on the see-through side but didn't want to appear ignorant as I seemed so pleased with my purchase and perhaps this was the future of swimwear?

No, it was one of the meanest girls at school who swam up to me in the pool during mixed free time and alerted me to the fact that my pubescent body might as well be naked. And though I couldn't get out of that pool and to the changing rooms fast enough, and though my family had to put up with an evening of tearful mortification, what I love about this memory is that my mother would attempt to sew strategically placed material inside the costume, and that my friends hadn't known where to look when I kept jumping off the side, but liked me too much to enlighten me.

Cities

Once in Leicester Square
a bird's wing touched my face.
It was just a London pigeon
whose spatial awareness
had gone out of kilter
but there was poetry in it.

And once on the Tokyo subway
on my way back to the airport
a Japanese commuter
wished me a good journey
home. How could I not
write such a thing down?

God's Own Junkyard

would be filled with illuminated
angel wings where one of the tubes
has gone. That's where I got the idea
for the name from. See that Circus sign?
That's one of my dad's. I had no interest
in learning the business until I saw
an exhibition of Bruce Nauman.
I too could be an artist of electricity.
But times were hard for fairgrounds
and they were slow to pay up.
This was the Sixties and I knew
where the money was, sex.
So I went to Soho. Not to have sex
but to spell it out in wattage.
Sex Sex Sex. Girls Girls Girls.
Fun Fun Fun. The power of three.
I set Soho on fire, literally. *Do you ever
dance with the devil in the pale moonlight?*
Jack Nicholson's line just before
he shot Batman in front of my blue
Hotel sign. I've been here for almost
forty years; it's the perfect spot,
the trains rattling past on their way
to Clacton. No small business
that makes things can compete
with the property developers.
I keep these signs to recycle.

LOVE: from the L of London
the O of Open, the V of Vacancies,
the E of Eternity. My father made
his neon in Walthamstow, I'm just
a bloke who wants to keep making
his neon in Walthamstow. I rage
against the dying of the light.

Romantic comedy

I had been worrying somewhat
about the final scene –
where to set it
and what could be the hero's
extravagant gesture?

But then I realised
how these things end.
He just shows up.
He just shows up
and says *I love you*.